Adaptive Harvest Management

2002 Duck Hunting Season

PREFACE

The process of setting waterfowl hunting regulations is conducted annually in the United States. This process involves a number of meetings where the status of waterfowl is reviewed by the agencies responsible for setting hunting regulations. In addition, the U.S. Fish and Wildlife Service (USFWS) publishes proposed regulations in the *Federal Register* to allow public comment. This document is part of a series of reports intended to support development of harvest regulations for the 2002 hunting season. Specifically, this report is intended to provide waterfowl managers and the public with information about the use of adaptive harvest management (AHM) for setting duck-hunting regulations in the United States. This report provides the most current data, analyses, and decision-making protocols. However, adaptive management is a dynamic process, and information presented in this report may differ from that in previous reports.

Citation:	U.S. Fish and Wildlife Service. 2002. Adaptive Harvest Management: 2002 Duck Hunting Season. U.S. Dept. Interior, Washington, D.C. 34pp.

ACKNOWLEDGMENTS

A working group comprised of technical representatives from the USFWS, the four Flyway Councils, and the U.S. Geological Survey (USGS) (Appendix A) was established in 1992 to review the scientific basis for managing waterfowl harvests. The working group subsequently proposed a framework of adaptive harvest management, which was first implemented in 1995. The USFWS expresses its gratitude to the AHM Working Group and other individuals, organizations, and agencies that have contributed to the development and implementation of AHM. We especially thank D. J. Case and Associates for help with information and education efforts.

This report was prepared by the USFWS Division of Migratory Bird Management. F. A. Johnson (USFWS) was the principal author, but significant contributions to the report were made by M. C. Runge (USGS Patuxent Wildlife Research Center), J. A. Dubovsky (USFWS), W. L. Kendall (USGS Patuxent Wildlife Research Center), and J. A. Royle (USFWS). D. J. Case (D.J. Case & Assoc.), R. Raftovich (USFWS), G. W. Smith (USFWS), and K. A. Wilkins (USFWS) provided essential information or otherwise assisted with report preparation. Comments or questions regarding this document should be sent to the Chief, Division of Migratory Bird Management - USFWS, Arlington Square, Room 634, 4401 North Fairfax Drive, Arlington, VA 22203.

Cover art:	Joseph Hautman's rendering of a black scoter (*Melanitta nigra*), which was selected for the 2002 federal "duck stamp." (The image has been reversed to function better as cover art for this report.)

TABLE OF CONTENTS

EXECUTIVE SUMMARY

In 1995, the USFWS adopted the concept of adaptive resource management for regulating duck harvests in the United States. The adaptive approach explicitly recognizes that the consequences of hunting regulations cannot be predicted with certainty, and provides a framework for making objective decisions in the face of that uncertainty.

The original AHM protocol was based solely on the dynamics of midcontinent mallards, but efforts are being made to account for mallards breeding eastward and westward of the midcontinent region. The challenge for managers is to vary hunting regulations among Flyways in a manner that recognizes each Flyway's unique breeding-ground derivation of mallards. For the 2002 hunting season, the USFWS will continue to consider a regulatory choice for the Atlantic Flyway that depends exclusively on the status of eastern mallards. This arrangement continues to be considered provisional, however, until the implications of this approach are better understood. The recommended regulatory choice for the Mississippi, Central, and Pacific Flyways continues to depend exclusively on the status of midcontinent mallards.

The population models upon which harvest regulations for midcontinent and eastern mallards are based have been in place since 1995 and 2000, respectively. However, the basic structure of the models, alternative hypotheses of population dynamics, and evidence associated with each hypothesis (i.e., model "weights") are subject to continuous review by parties both internal and external to the AHM process. This year, some important revisions have been made to these protocols. Most notably, empirical corrections have been made for the +11% and +16% bias in estimated growth rates of midcontinent and eastern mallards, respectively. The procedure for updating model weights also has been revised to include all sources of prediction error, including those not accounted for by the models of survival and reproductive rates. In addition, the eastern-mallard protocol now relies solely on federal and state waterfowl surveys to index breeding-population size, and includes competing hypotheses of strongly and weakly density-dependent reproduction.

For the 2002 season, the USFWS is maintaining the same regulatory alternatives as those used during 1997-2001, except that opening and closing framework dates have been extended in the moderate and liberal alternatives. Based on a recommendation from the AHM Working Group, the USFWS has adopted Bayesian statistical methods for generating predictions of harvest rates associated with these alternatives. Essentially, the idea is to use existing ("prior") information to develop initial harvest-rate predictions, to make regulatory decisions based on those predictions, and then to observe realized harvest rates. Those observed harvest rates, in turn, are treated as new sources of information for calculating updated ("posterior") predictions. Using this approach, predictions of harvest rates of midcontinent mallards under the liberal regulatory alternative have been updated based on reward banding during 1998-2001. The initial prediction about extended framework dates is that they will increase harvest rates by 15% and 5% for midcontinent and eastern mallards, respectively.

Optimal regulatory choices for the 2002 hunting season were calculated using: (1) stock-specific harvest-management objectives; (2) the revised regulatory alternatives for 2002; and (3) the revised population models and associated weights for midcontinent and eastern mallards. Based on this year's survey results of 8.53 million midcontinent mallards (traditional surveys plus state surveys in MN, WI, and MI), 1.44 million ponds in Prairie Canada, and 1.0 million eastern mallards, the recommended regulatory choice for all Flyways is the liberal alternative.

The USFWS is continuing discussions with the AHM Working Group, Flyway Councils, States, and others about future development and application of AHM. The USFWS has decided to convene a task force, comprised of recognized state and federal leaders in waterfowl management, to help provide policy guidance regarding the nature of harvest management objectives and regulatory alternatives. Moreover, it is apparent that the future success of AHM will depend on how managers account for variation in the ability of different duck species to support harvest without adverse impact. An effective means to account for these differences in the face of a common duck-hunting season is a high priority for the task force and AHM Working Group.

BACKGROUND

The annual process of setting duck-hunting regulations in the United States is based on a system of resource monitoring, data analyses, and rule making (Blohm 1989). Each year, monitoring activities such as aerial surveys and hunter questionnaires provide information on harvest levels, population size, and habitat conditions. Data collected from this monitoring program are analyzed each year, and proposals for duck-hunting regulations are developed by the Flyway Councils, States, and USFWS. After extensive public review, the USFWS announces a regulatory framework within which States can set their hunting seasons.

In 1995, the USFWS adopted the concept of adaptive resource management (Walters 1986) for regulating duck harvests in the United States. The adaptive approach explicitly recognizes that the consequences of hunting regulations cannot be predicted with certainty, and provides a framework for making objective decisions in the face of that uncertainty (Williams and Johnson 1995). Inherent in the adaptive approach is an awareness that management performance can be maximized only if regulatory effects can be predicted reliably. Thus, adaptive management relies on an iterative cycle of monitoring, assessment, and decision making to clarify the relationships among hunting regulations, harvests, and waterfowl abundance.

In regulating waterfowl harvests, managers face four fundamental sources of uncertainty (Nichols et al. 1995, Johnson et al. 1996, Williams et al. 1996):

(1)   environmental variation - the temporal and spatial variation in weather conditions and other key features of waterfowl habitat; an example is the annual change in the number of ponds in the Prairie Pothole Region, where water conditions influence duck reproductive success;

(2)   partial controllability - the ability of managers to control harvest only within limits; the harvest resulting from a particular set of hunting regulations cannot be predicted with certainty because of variation in weather conditions, timing of migration, hunter effort, and other factors;

(3)   partial observability - the ability to estimate key population attributes (e.g., population size, reproductive rate, harvest) only within the precision afforded by existing monitoring programs; and

(4)   structural uncertainty - an incomplete understanding of biological processes; a familiar example is the long-standing debate about whether harvest is additive to other sources of mortality or whether populations compensate for hunting losses through reduced natural mortality. Structural uncertainty increases contentiousness in the decision-making process and decreases the extent to which managers can meet long-term conservation goals.

AHM was developed as a systematic process for dealing objectively with these uncertainties. The key components of AHM (Johnson et al. 1993, Williams and Johnson 1995) include:

(1)   a limited number of regulatory alternatives, which describe Flyway-specific season lengths, bag limits, and framework dates;

(2)   a set of population models describing various hypotheses about the effects of harvest and environmental factors on waterfowl abundance;

(3)   a measure of reliability (probability or "weight") for each population model; and

(4)   a mathematical description of the objective(s) of harvest management (i.e., an "objective function"), by which alternative regulatory strategies can be evaluated.

These components are used in a stochastic optimization procedure to derive a regulatory strategy. A regulatory strategy specifies the optimal regulatory choice, with respect to the stated objectives of management, for each possible combination of breeding population size, environmental conditions, and model weights (Johnson et al. 1997). The setting of annual hunting regulations then involves an iterative process:

(1)   each year, an optimal regulatory alternative is identified based on resource and environmental conditions, and on current model weights;

(2)   after the regulatory decision is made, model-specific predictions for subsequent breeding population size are determined;

(3)   when monitoring data become available, model weights are increased to the extent that observations of population size agree with predictions, and decreased to the extent that they disagree; and

(4)   the new model weights are used to start another iteration of the process.

By iteratively updating model weights and optimizing regulatory choices, the process should eventually identify which model is the best overall predictor of changes in abundance of the managed population. The process is optimal in the sense that it provides the regulatory choice each year necessary to maximize management performance. It is adaptive in the sense that the harvest strategy "evolves" to account for new knowledge generated by a comparison of predicted and observed population sizes.

MALLARD STOCKS AND FLYWAY MANAGEMENT

Significant numbers of breeding mallards occur from the northern U.S. through Canada and into Alaska. Geographic differences in the reproduction, mortality, and migrations of these mallards suggest that there are corresponding differences in optimal levels of sport harvest. The ability to regulate harvests of mallards originating from various breeding areas is complicated, however, by the fact that a large degree of mixing occurs during the hunting season. The challenge for managers, then, is to vary hunting regulations among Flyways in a manner that recognizes each Flyway's unique breeding-ground derivation of mallards. Of course, no Flyway receives mallards exclusively from one breeding area, and so Flyway-specific harvest strategies ideally must account for multiple breeding stocks that are exposed to a common harvest.

The optimization procedures used in AHM can account for breeding populations of mallards beyond the midcontinent region, and for the manner in which these ducks distribute themselves among the Flyways during the hunting season. An optimal approach would allow for Flyway-specific regulatory strategies, which in a sense represent for each Flyway an average of the optimal harvest strategies for each contributing breeding stock, weighted by the relative size of each stock in the fall flight. This "joint optimization" of multiple mallard stocks requires:

(1)   models of population dynamics for all recognized stocks of mallards;

(2)   an objective function that accounts for harvest-management goals for all mallard stocks in the aggregate; and

(3)   modification of the decision rules to allow independent regulatory choices among the Flyways.

Joint optimization of multiple stocks presents many challenges in terms of modeling, parameter estimation, and computation of regulatory strategies. These challenges cannot always be overcome due to limitations in monitoring and assessment programs, and in access to sufficient computing resources. In some cases, it is possible to impose constraints or assumptions that simplify the problem. Although sub-optimal by design, these constrained regulatory strategies may perform nearly as well as those that are optimal, particularly in cases where breeding stocks differ little in their ability to support harvest, where Flyways don't receive significant numbers of birds from more than one breeding stock, or where management outcomes are highly uncertain.

Currently, two stocks of mallards are officially recognized for the purposes of AHM (Fig. 1). We continue to use a constrained approach to the optimization of these stocks' harvest, whereby the Atlantic Flyway regulatory strategy is based exclusively on the status of eastern mallards, and the regulatory strategy for the remaining Flyways is based exclusively on the status of midcontinent mallards. This approach has been determined to perform nearly as well as a joint-optimization approach because mixing of the two stocks during the hunting season is limited. However, the approach continues to be considered provisional until its implications are better understood.

MALLARD POPULATION DYNAMICS

Midcontinent Mallards

For the purposes of AHM, midcontinent mallards are defined as those breeding in federal survey strata 1-18, 20-50, and 75-77 (i.e., the "traditional" survey area), and in Minnesota, Wisconsin, and Michigan. Estimates of the midcontinent population so defined are available only since 1992 (Table 1).

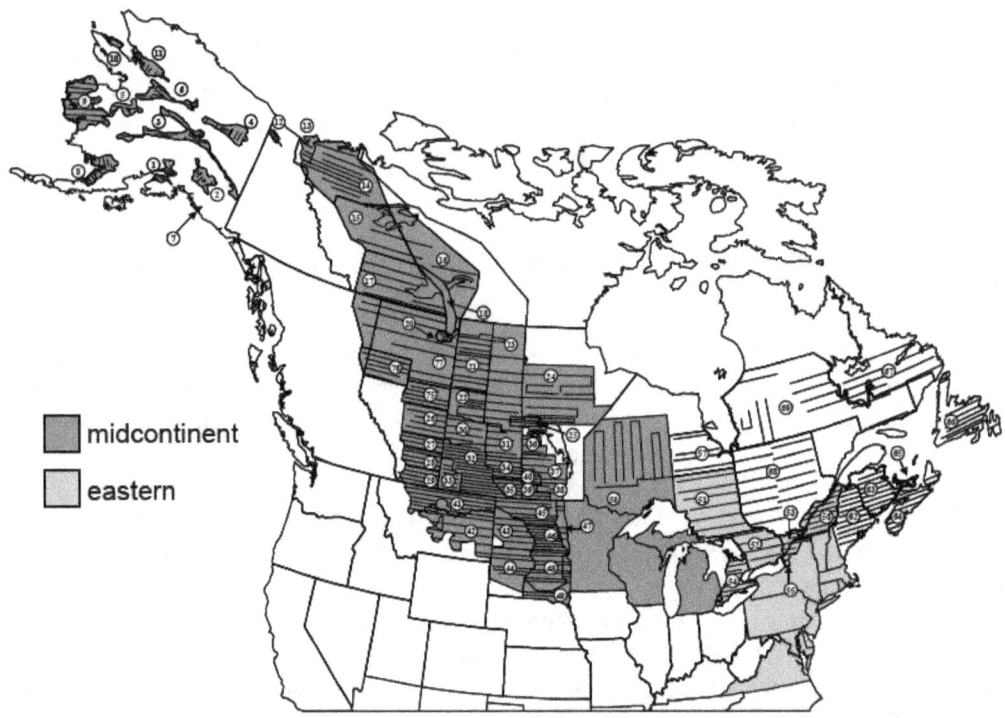

Fig. 1. Survey areas currently assigned to the midcontinent and eastern stocks of mallards for the purposes of AHM. Delineation of the western-mallard stock is pending a review of population monitoring programs.

Table 1. Estimates (N) and associated standard errors (SE) of mallards (in thousands) in spring in the traditional survey area (strata 1-18, 20-50, and 75-77) and the states of Minnesota, Wisconsin, and Michigan.

Year	Traditional surveys		State surveys		Total	
	N	SE	N	SE	N	SE
1992	5976.1	241.0	977.9	118.7	6954.0	268.6
1993	5708.3	208.9	863.5	100.5	6571.8	231.8
1994	6980.1	282.8	1103.0	138.8	8083.1	315.0
1995	8269.4	287.5	1052.2	130.6	9321.6	304.5
1996	7941.3	262.9	945.7	81.0	8887.0	275.1
1997	9939.7	308.5	1026.1	91.2	10965.8	321.7
1998	9640.4	301.6	979.6	88.4	10620.0	314.3
1999	10805.7	344.5	957.5	100.6	11763.1	358.9
2000	9470.2	290.2	1031.1	85.3	10501.3	302.5
2001	7904.0	226.9	779.7	59.0	8683.7	234.5
2002	7503.7	246.5	1029.6	78.0	8533.3	258.5

The dynamics of midcontinent mallards are described by four alternative models, which result from combining two mortality and two reproductive hypotheses (Johnson et al. 1997). Collectively, the models express uncertainty (or disagreement) about whether harvest is an additive or compensatory form of mortality (Burnham et al. 1984), and whether the reproductive process is weakly or strongly density dependent (i.e., the degree to which reproductive rates decline with increasing population size). The model with additive hunting mortality and weakly density-dependent recruitment (SaRw) leads to the most conservative harvest strategy, whereas the model with compensatory hunting mortality and strongly density-dependent recruitment (ScRs) leads to the most liberal strategy. The other two models (SaRs and ScRw) lead to strategies that are intermediate between these extremes.

The population models upon which harvest regulations for midcontinent mallards are based have been in place since implementation of AHM in 1995. However, the basic structure of the models, the alternative hypotheses of population dynamics, and the evidence associated with each hypothesis (i.e., model "weights") are subject to continuous review by parties both internal and external to the AHM process. Over the last two years the AHM Working Group has focused on two especially important concerns about the models for midcontinent mallards:

(1) <u>Apparent bias in estimates of reproductive or survival rates</u> – The population models for midcontinent mallards share a common structure referred to as the balance equation. The balance equation is essentially an accounting tool, which predicts population size in a given year based on population size (N), reproduction (R), and survival (S) from the previous year. In theory, N, R, and S from a given year should perfectly predict N the next year. In fact, they do not (Fig. 2). Predicted population sizes are 11% higher on average than those observed in the population surveys. The bias is not related to the nature of any predictive models, but to estimates of survival and reproductive rates derived from resource monitoring programs. Those programs are now being carefully scrutinized for the source and cause of the bias.

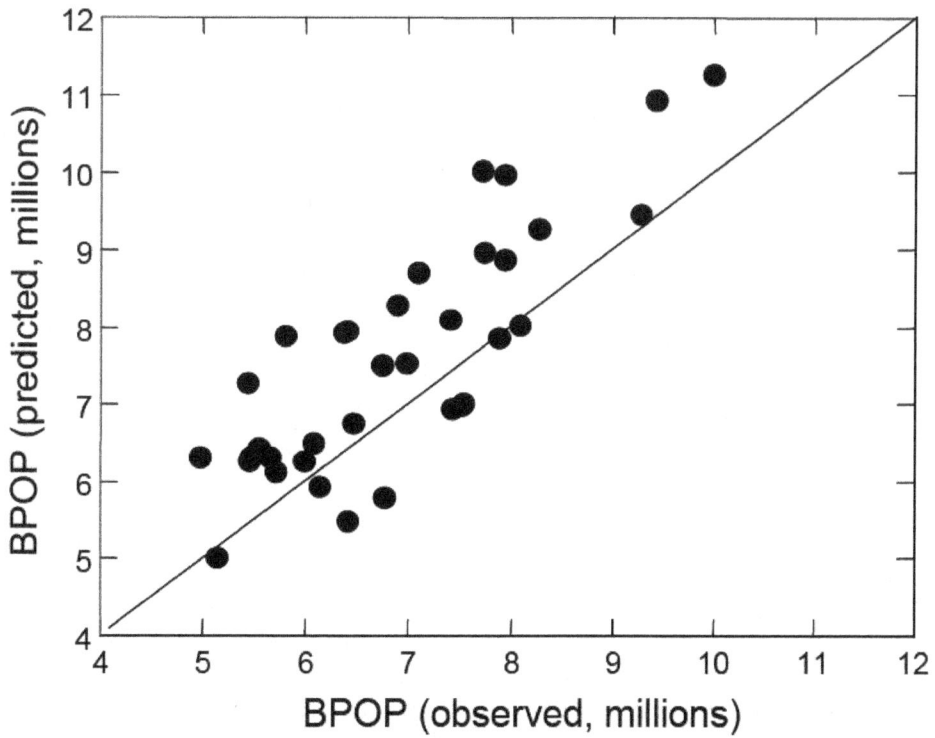

Fig. 2. Predicted versus observed breeding-population size (BPOP) for midcontinent mallards in the traditional survey area, 1962-1996. Predictions were generated using the balance equation and uncorrected estimates of survival and reproductive rates.

(2) <u>Updating model weights</u> – The purpose of annually updating model weights is to eventually identify the model providing the most accurate predictions over time, based on a comparison of the observed population size with those predicted under

each alternative model. Model weights are highly influential in determining optimal harvest strategies because they determine the degree to which a single set of biological hypotheses (i.e., a particular model) dominates the optimization. The AHM Working Group has determined that the procedure for updating model weights used since 1995 is inadequate because of the omission of certain random errors common to all predictive models. The inclusion of these prediction errors in the updating procedure will minimize the chances of major shifts of model weights in any single year, and help ensure that model weights more accurately reflect the evidence in support of the alternative hypotheses (Johnson et al. 2002b).

Based on recommendations from the AHM Working Group, the USFWS has made revisions to the AHM protocol for midcontinent mallards to address the concerns described above. These revisions involve empirical corrections to all models for the +11% bias in population growth rates, and modification of the updating procedure to include all sources of prediction error, including those not accounted for by the sub-models of survival and reproductive rates. In addition, a number of other noteworthy revisions were made:

(a)   The alternative survival hypotheses were re-parameterized to better reflect the uncertainty about survival rates in the absence of hunting.
(b)   The alternative hypotheses of reproduction were chosen so that they were equally supported by the available data (this was not the case for the models specified by Johnson et al. [1997]).
(c)   The dynamic model for Canadian ponds was revised to predict ponds in year $t+1$ as a function of ponds in year t and random error from all sources. Annual precipitation was dropped as a predictor and its contribution to variation in ponds is now included in a residual error term.

We derived optimal harvest strategies for each of the revised models using stochastic dynamic programming (Lubow 1995), conditioning on the 2001 set of regulatory alternatives (i.e., without framework-date extensions) and the current objective function (see the sections on Harvest-Management Objectives and Regulatory Alternatives later in this report). We also simulated these strategies to understand their expected dynamics.

Under the models with compensatory hunting mortality (ScRs and ScRw), the optimal strategy is to have a liberal regulation regardless of population size or number of ponds because at harvest rates achieved under the liberal alternative, harvest has no effect on population size (Fig. 3). Under the strongly density-dependent model (ScRs), the density-dependence regulates the population and keeps it within narrow bounds. Under the weakly density-dependent model (ScRw), the density-dependence does not exert as strong a regulatory effect, and the population size fluctuates more.

The optimal strategies associated with the models with additive hunting mortality (SaRs and SaRw) are more conservative because hunting regulations can have a pronounced effect on population size and, thus, on the ability to maintain the mallard population above the goal of the North American Waterfowl Management Plan (NAWMP). The strategy associated with the strongly density-dependent reproductive model (SaRs) is considerably more liberal, however, than that associated with the weakly density-dependent model (SaRw). Average population size is expected to be slightly higher under the model with weakly density-dependent reproduction (SaRw).

The revisions to the AHM protocol for midcontinent mallards have produced different conclusions about the best predictive models than those published previously (USFWS 2001, Johnson et al. 2002b). Using the revised protocol, model weights suggest much less evidence for the hypotheses of additive hunting mortality and strongly density-dependent reproduction than had been the case with the old protocol (Table 2). Under the old protocol, the model that accumulated the most weight (SaRs) was the one that best compensated for the positive bias in projected growth rates (i.e., the model that predicted the lowest growth rate provided the most accurate predictions because growth rates from all of the old models were biased high). This self-regulating mechanism helped ensure that regulations in the past were commensurate with resource status, even in the face of an uncorrected bias in growth rates. This example also illustrates why models can sometimes make reliable predictions of population size for reasons having little to do with the biological hypotheses expressed therein (Johnson et al. 2002b).

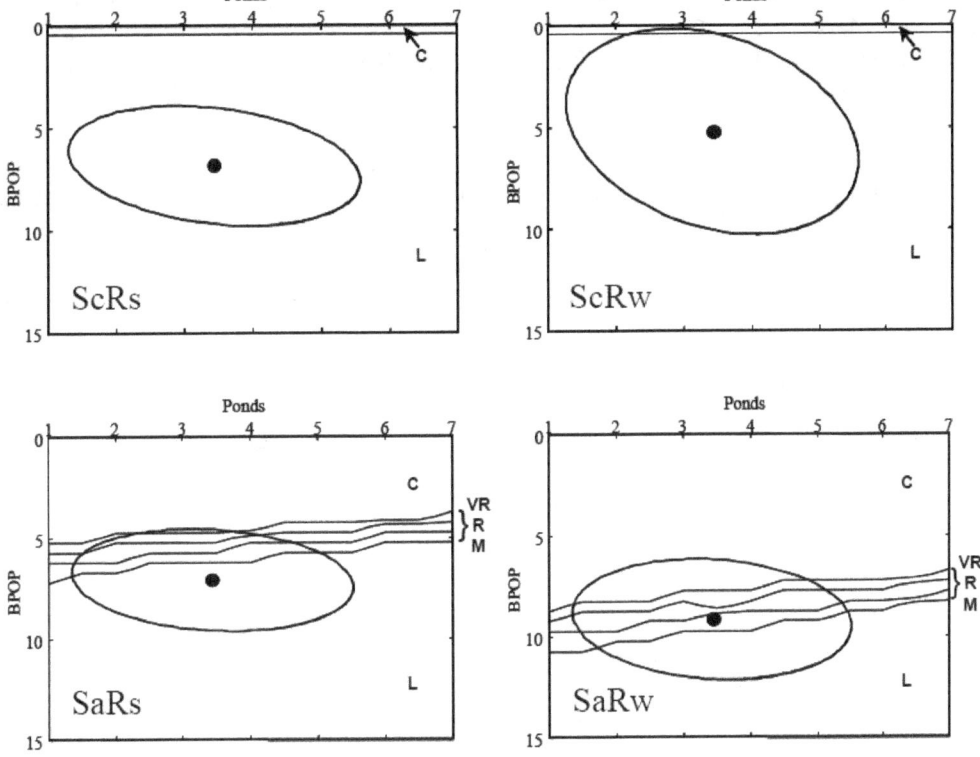

Fig. 3. Model-specific, optimal regulatory strategies for midcontinent mallards conditioned on population size (BPOP) and ponds in Prairie Canada. These strategies are based on the current harvest-management objective and the 2001 set of regulatory alternatives (ScRs = compensatory mortality and strongly density-dependent reproduction, ScRw = compensatory mortality and weakly density-dependent reproduction, SaRs = additive mortality and strongly density-dependent reproduction, and SaRw = additive mortality and weakly density-dependent reproduction) (C = closed season, VR = very restrictive, R = restrictive, M = moderate, and L = liberal). The dot in the center of each figure represents predicted mean population size and pond numbers under the model-specific strategy, and the ellipse represents conditions expected in 95% of all years.

Table 2. Weights for the revised models of midcontinent mallards (ScRs = compensatory mortality and strongly density-dependent reproduction, ScRw = compensatory mortality and weakly density-dependent reproduction, SaRs = additive mortality and strongly density-dependent reproduction, and SaRw = additive mortality and weakly density-dependent reproduction). Model weights were assumed to be equal in 1995.

	Model			
Year	ScRs	ScRw	SaRs	SaRw
1996	0.2469	0.2525	0.2481	0.2524
1997	0.2299	0.2659	0.2353	0.2688
1998	0.2244	0.2733	0.2220	0.2804
1999	0.0600	0.3826	0.0872	0.4702
2000	0.0551	0.4030	0.0910	0.4509
2001	0.0517	0.4052	0.0863	0.4568
2002	0.0461	0.4056	0.0823	0.4660

The revised models and weights for midcontinent mallards have good predictive ability (Table 3). Although the variance of predicted population sizes is large, the point predictions differ from the observations by only 6% on average. The relatively large discrepancies in some years (1997 and 1999) likely are indicative of important environmental factors influencing population dynamics that are not included in the current set of models.

Table 3. Observed and predicted population sizes (N, in millions) of midcontinent mallards in the traditional survey area. Predicted population sizes were calculated using the revised models of population dynamics to generate model-specific predictions, and then these predictions were averaged using annual model weights.

| | Predictor variables | | | N in subsequent year | | | |
| | | | | Predicted | | Observed | |
Year	N	Ponds	Harvest rate	N	SE(N)	N	% difference
1995	8.269	3.892	0.120	7.854	1.324	7.941	-1.10
1996	7.941	5.003	0.118	8.126	1.370	9.940	-18.25
1997	9.940	5.061	0.131	9.466	1.596	9.640	-1.80
1998	9.640	2.522	0.112	8.093	1.364	10.806	-25.11
1999	10.806	3.862	0.101	9.971	1.681	9.470	+5.29
2000	9.470	2.422	0.127	8.143	1.373	7.904	+3.02
2001	7.904	2.747	0.109	7.299	1.231	7.504	-2.73

A complete description of the revisions to the AHM protocol for midcontinent mallards is beyond the scope of this document, so we encourage the reader to examine the technical report prepared by Runge et al. (2002). A copy of this report can be obtained online at http://migratorybirds.fws.gov/reports/ahm02/MCMrevise2002.pdf.

Eastern Mallards

For purposes of AHM, eastern mallards are defined as those breeding in southern Ontario and Quebec (federal survey strata 51-54 and 56) and in the northeastern U.S. (state plot surveys; Heusmann and Sauer 2000) (Fig. 1). Estimates of population size have varied from 856 thousand to 1.1 million since 1990, with the majority of the population accounted for in the northeastern U.S. (Table 4).

Last year, the USFWS (2001) described several reasons that revisions to the existing AHM protocol for eastern mallards might be warranted. First, it was believed that the number of existing models might be reduced because differences in model-specific regulatory strategies were relatively minor. Another motivation concerned the tendency for empirical estimates of survival and reproductive rates of eastern mallards to imply annual growth rates that are higher than those observed in surveys of population size (as in midcontinent mallards). Finally, the Breeding Bird Survey (BBS) index used to predict reproductive success of eastern mallards appeared to be biased low in years of high spring precipitation.

Based on recommendations from the AHM Working Group, the USFWS has revised the AHM protocol for eastern mallards. A revised set of six models: (1) rely solely on federal and state waterfowl surveys rather than the BBS to predict reproductive rates; (2) allow for the possibility of a positive bias in estimates of survival or reproductive rates; (3) incorporate competing hypotheses of strongly and weakly density-dependent reproduction; and (4) assume that hunting mortality is additive to other sources of mortality. We retained models with no bias-correction in the final model set because the time-series available for comparing observed and predicted population sizes was relatively short. For the bias-corrected models, we allowed for the possibility that the bias resides either in estimates of survival or reproductive rates.

Table 4. Estimates (N) and associated standard errors (SE) of mallards (in thousands) in spring in the northeastern U.S. (state plot surveys) and eastern Canada (federal survey strata 51-54 and 56).

Year	State surveys		Federal surveys		Total	
	N	SE	N	SE	N	SE
1990	665.1	78.3	190.7	47.2	855.8	91.4
1991	779.2	88.3	152.8	33.7	932.0	94.5
1992	562.2	47.9	320.3	53.0	882.5	71.5
1993	683.1	49.7	292.1	48.2	975.2	69.3
1994	853.1	62.7	219.5	28.2	1072.5	68.7
1995	862.8	70.2	184.4	40.0	1047.2	80.9
1996	848.4	61.1	283.1	55.7	1131.5	82.6
1997	795.1	49.6	212.1	39.6	1007.2	63.4
1998	775.1	49.7	263.8	67.2	1038.9	83.6
1999	879.7	60.2	212.5	36.9	1092.2	70.6
2000	757.8	48.5	132.3	26.4	890.0	55.2
2001	807.5	51.4	200.2	35.6	1007.7	62.5
2002	834.1	56.2	171.3	30.0	1005.4	63.8

We derived optimal harvest strategies for each of the six models using stochastic dynamic programming (Lubow 1995), and by conditioning on the current set of regulatory alternatives and a management objective to maximize long-term cumulative harvest. Equilibrium population sizes were determined by simulating the optimal strategy with the model that gave rise to it. The model-specific strategies based on the hypothesis of weakly density-dependent reproduction appear to be considerably more conservative than those based on the hypothesis of strongly density-dependent reproduction (Table 5). All harvest strategies are "knife-edged," meaning that large differences in the optimal regulatory alternative can be precipitated by only small changes in breeding-population size. This result is largely due to the small differences in predicted harvest rates among the current regulatory alternatives (see the section on Regulatory Alternatives later in this report).

For the first time, we have calculated weights for the alternative models of eastern mallard population dynamics, based on an assumption of equal model weights in 1996 (the last year data was used to develop most model components) and on predictions of year-specific harvest rates. The model best predicting observed population size has varied among years; accordingly, there is no single model that is clearly favored over the others at the end of the time frame (Table 6). However, we note that the two models with no bias correction performed poorly compared to the models with a bias correction.

As with midcontinent mallards, a detailed description of the revisions to the AHM protocol for eastern mallards is beyond the scope of this document. Therefore, we encourage the reader to examine the technical report prepared by Johnson et al. (2002a). A copy of this report can be obtained online at http://migratorybirds.fws.gov/reports/ahm02/emal-ahm-2002.pdf.

Western Mallards

Western mallards occur in the states of the Pacific Flyway (including Alaska), British Columbia, and the Yukon Territory during the breeding season. The distribution of these mallards during fall and winter is centered in the Pacific Flyway (Munro and Kimball 1982). Unfortunately, data-collection programs for understanding and monitoring the dynamics of this mallard stock are highly fragmented in both time and space. This fact is making it difficult to aggregate monitoring instruments in

Table 5. Model-specific, optimal regulatory strategies for eastern mallards based on the current set of regulatory alternatives and an objective to maximize long-term cumulative harvest. The average population size expected under each model and accompanying strategy is represented by the shaded cells. (BPOP = breeding-population size in millions) (BnRw = no bias-correction and weakly density-dependent reproduction, BnRs = no bias-correction and strongly density-dependent reproduction, BsRw = bias-corrected survival rates and weakly density-dependent reproduction, BsRs = bias-corrected survival rates and strongly density-dependent reproduction, BrRw = bias-corrected reproductive rates and weakly density-dependent reproduction, and BrRs = bias-corrected reproductive rates and strongly density-dependent reproduction).

	Model					
BPOP	BnRw	BnRs	BsRw	BsRs	BrRw	BrRs
0.1	C	C	C	C	C	C
0.2	C	L	C	L	C	VR
0.3	C	L	C	L	C	L
0.4	C	L	C	L	C	L
0.5	C	L	C	L	C	L
0.6	C	L	C	L	C	L
0.7	C	L	C	L	C	L
0.8	C	L	C	L	C	L
0.9	C	L	C	L	C	L
1.0	C	L	VR	L	C	L
1.1	C	L	M	L	VR	L
1.2	R	L	L	L	R	L
1.3	M	L	L	L	L	L
1.4	L	L	L	L	L	L
1.5	L	L	L	L	L	L

Table 6. Weights for the revised models of eastern mallards. (BnRw = no bias-correction and weakly density-dependent reproduction, BnRs = no bias-correction and strongly density-dependent reproduction, BsRw = bias-corrected survival rates and weakly density-dependent reproduction, BsRs = bias-corrected survival rates and strongly density-dependent reproduction, BrRw = bias-corrected reproductive rates and weakly density-dependent reproduction, and BrRs = bias-corrected reproductive rates and strongly density-dependent reproduction). Model weights were assumed to be equal in 1996.

	Model					
Year	BnRw	BnRs	BsRw	BsRs	BrRw	BrRs
1997	0.0565	0.1100	0.2053	0.2129	0.1996	0.2157
1998	0.0775	0.1515	0.1855	0.1897	0.1913	0.2045
1999	0.1257	0.2489	0.1552	0.1344	0.1732	0.1627
2000	0.0297	0.1066	0.2042	0.2068	0.2153	0.2374
2001	0.0553	0.1932	0.1270	0.2303	0.1408	0.2533
2002	0.0585	0.2062	0.1223	0.2190	0.1416	0.2524

a way that can be used to reliably model this stock's dynamics and, thus, to establish criteria for regulatory decision-making under AHM (USFWS 2001). Another complicating factor is that federal survey strata 1-12 in Alaska and the Yukon are within the current geographic bounds of midcontinent mallards. Therefore, the AHM Working Group is continuing its investigations of western mallards and is not prepared to recommend an AHM protocol at this time.

HARVEST MANAGEMENT OBJECTIVES

The basic harvest-management objective for midcontinent mallards is to maximize cumulative harvest over the long term, which inherently requires perpetuation of a viable population. Moreover, this objective is constrained to avoid regulations that could be expected to result in a subsequent population size below the goal of the NAWMP (Fig. 4). According to this constraint, the value of harvest decreases proportionally as the difference between the goal and expected population size increases. This balance of harvest and population objectives results in a regulatory strategy that is more conservative than that for maximizing long-term harvest, but more liberal than a strategy to attain the NAWMP goal (regardless of effects on hunting opportunity). The current objective uses a population goal of 8.799 million mallards, which is based on 8.199 million mallards in the traditional survey area (from the 1998 update of the NAWMP) and a goal of 0.6 million for the combined states of Minnesota, Wisconsin, and Michigan.

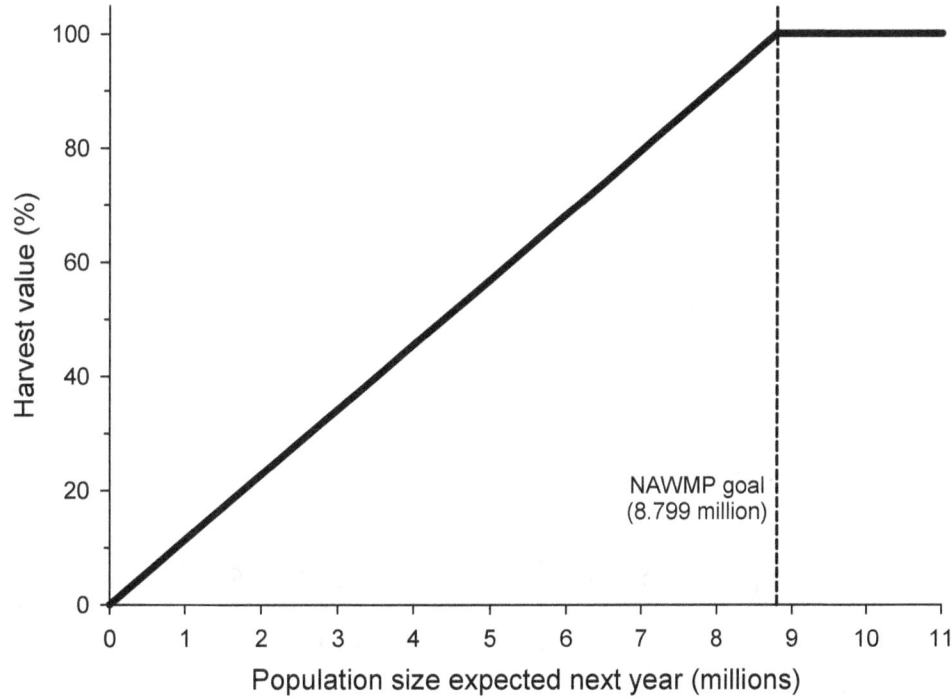

For eastern mallards, there is no NAWMP goal or other established target for desired population size. Accordingly, the management objective for eastern mallards is simply to maximize long-term cumulative harvest.

REGULATORY ALTERNATIVES

Evolution of Alternatives

When AHM was first implemented in 1995, three regulatory alternatives characterized as liberal, moderate, and restrictive were defined based on regulations used during 1979-84, 1985-87, and 1988-93, respectively (Appendix B). These regulatory alternatives also were considered for the 1996 hunting season. In 1997, the regulatory alternatives were modified to include: (1) the addition of a very restrictive alternative; (2) additional days and a higher duck bag limit in the moderate and liberal alternatives; and (3) an increase in the bag limit of hen mallards in the moderate and liberal alternatives. This year, the USFWS further modified the moderate and liberal alternatives to include extensions of approximately one week in both the opening and closing framework dates (Table 7).

Table 7. Regulatory alternatives considered for the 2002 duck-hunting season.

Regulation	Flyway			
	Atlantic[a]	Mississippi	Central[b]	Pacific[c]
Shooting hours	one-half hour before sunrise to sunset			
Framework dates				
Very restrictive and Restrictive	Oct 1 - Jan 20	Saturday nearest Oct 1 - Sunday nearest Jan 20		
Moderate and Liberal	Saturday nearest Sep 24 - last Sunday in Jan			
Season length (days)				
Very restrictive	20	20	25	38
Restrictive	30	30	39	60
Moderate	45	45	60	86
Liberal	60	60	74	107
Bag limit (total / mallard / female mallard)				
Very restrictive	3 / 3 / 1	3 / 2 / 1	3 / 3 / 1	4 / 3 / 1
Restrictive	3 / 3 / 1	3 / 2 / 1	3 / 3 / 1	4 / 3 / 1
Moderate	6 / 4 / 2	6 / 4 / 1	6 / 5 / 1	7 / 5 / 2
Liberal	6 / 4 / 2	6 / 4 / 2	6 / 5 / 2	7 / 7 / 2

[a] The states of Maine, Massachusetts, Connecticut, Pennsylvania, New Jersey, Maryland, Delaware, West Virginia, Virginia, and North Carolina are permitted to exclude Sundays, which are closed to hunting, from their total allotment of season days.
[b] The High Plains Mallard Management Unit is allowed 8, 12, 23, and 23 extra days in the very restrictive, restrictive, moderate, and liberal alternatives, respectively.
[c] The Columbia Basin Mallard Management Unit is allowed seven extra days in the very restrictive, restrictive, and moderate alternatives.

Predictions of Mallard Harvest Rates

Since 1995, harvest rates of adult male mallards associated with the regulatory alternatives have been predicted using harvest-rate estimates from 1979-84, which have been adjusted to reflect current specifications of season lengths and bag limits, and for contemporary numbers of hunters. These predictions are based only in part on band-recovery data, and rely heavily on models of hunting effort and success derived from hunter surveys (Appendix C). As such, these predictions have large sampling variances, and their accuracy is uncertain. Moreover, these predictions rely implicitly on an assumption that the historic relationship between hunting regulations (and harvest rates) in the U.S. and Canada will remain unchanged in the future. Currently, we have no way to judge whether this is a reasonable assumption. We also assumed that if hunting seasons were closed in the U.S., rates of harvest in Canada would be similar to those observed during 1988-93, which is the most recent period for which reliable estimates from Canada are available. This is a conservative approach given that we cannot be sure Canada would close its hunting season at the same time as the U.S. Fortunately, optimal regulatory strategies do not appear to be very sensitive to what we believe to be a realistic range of harvest-rate values associated with closed seasons in the U.S.

We have adopted standard Bayesian statistical methods for improving regulation-specific predictions of harvest rates, including predictions of the effects of framework-date extensions (Appendix D). Essentially, the idea is to use existing ("prior") information to develop initial harvest-rate predictions (as above), to make regulatory decisions based on those predictions, and then to observe realized harvest rates. Those observed harvest rates, in turn, are treated as new sources of information for calculating updated ("posterior") predictions. Bayesian methods are attractive because they provide a quantitative and formal, yet intuitive, model with which to express an adaptive approach to management. In this approach, we rely on the following model structure:

$$h_t \sim Normal\left(\mu + \Delta, v^2\right)$$

where h_t is the harvest rate realized under a particular regulatory alternative in any year t. These rates are assumed to be normally distributed with mean $\mu + \Delta$ and variance v^2. In this statistical model, μ is the mean harvest rate expected in the absence of framework-date extensions, Δ is the marginal change in mean harvest rate associated with extended framework dates, and v^2 is the amount of annual variability in harvest rate due to uncontrolled environmental factors and changes in hunter effort. For prior estimates of μ, we relied on the regulation-specific estimates of mean harvest rates provided by the USFWS (2000a:13-14) under the assumption of uniform regulatory choices across Flyways. Based on analyses by Johnson et al. (1997), we assumed that v averages 20% of the mean. Updated predictions of midcontinent mallard harvest rates under the liberal alternative (without framework-date extensions) were calculated based on observed harvest rates during the 1998-2001 hunting seasons that were estimated with data from a small-scale reward-band study (Appendix D).

A previous analysis by the USFWS (2000b) suggested that implementation of framework-date extensions might be expected to increase harvest by 15% and 5% for midcontinent and eastern mallards, respectively. Accordingly, we used a prior mean of $\Delta = 0.02$ for midcontinent mallards and $\Delta = 0.01$ for eastern mallards. However, there is a great deal of uncertainty about the magnitude of the increases because of a lack of prior experience with nationwide extensions. Therefore, we explicitly recognized this uncertainty in deriving optimal harvest strategies. The measures of uncertainty (i.e., the variances of Δ) we used were large enough to admit the possibility that extensions will result in *no* increase in mean harvest rates. After framework-date extensions have been implemented, estimates of harvest rate derived from band-recovery data will be used to update the estimate of Δ (the marginal effect of extensions). However, strong inference about Δ depends on reliable knowledge of μ (which is lacking in some cases), and on an experimental study design (which is likely not feasible).

Predicted harvest rates of adult male mallards associated with each of the regulatory alternatives are provided in Tables 8 and 9 and Figs. 5 and 6. We made the simplifying assumption that the harvest rate of midcontinent mallards depends solely on the regulatory choice in the western three Flyways. This appears to be a reasonable assumption given the the small proportion of midcontinent mallards wintering in the Atlantic Flyway (Munro and Kimball 1982), and harvest-rate predictions that suggest a minimal effect of Atlantic Flyway regulations (USFWS 2000a). Under this assumption, the optimal regulatory strategy for the western three Flyways can be derived by ignoring the harvest regulations imposed in the Atlantic Flyway. However, the harvest rate of eastern mallards is affected significantly by regulatory choices beyond the Atlantic Flyway USFWS 2000a). To avoid making the regulatory choice in the Atlantic Flyway conditional on regulations elsewhere, we inflated the variance of predicted harvest rates of eastern mallards to account for uncontrolled changes in regulations in the three western Flyways (Johnson et al. 2002a).

Harvest rates of age and sex cohorts other than adult male mallards are based on constant rates of differential vulnerability as derived from band-recovery data. For midcontinent mallards, these constants are 0.719, 1.541, and 1.118 for adult females, young males, and young females, respectively. For eastern mallards, these constants are 1.153, 1.331, and 1.509 for adult females, young males, and young females, respectively.

15

Table 8. Predicted harvest rates of adult male midcontinent mallards based on regulations in the three western Flyways. The parameter μ is the mean harvest rate expected in the absence of framework-date extensions and Δ is the marginal change in mean harvest rate expected with extended framework dates. Standard errors are in parentheses.

Regulatory alternative	μ	Δ	$\mu + \Delta$
Closed (U.S.)	0.0088 (0.0018)	N/A	
Very restrictive	0.0526 (0.0105)	N/A	
Restrictive	0.0665 (0.0133)	N/A	
Moderate	0.1114 (0.0223)	0.02 (0.01)	0.1314 (0.0244)
Liberal	0.1210 (0.0222)	0.02 (0.01)	0.1410 (0.0243)

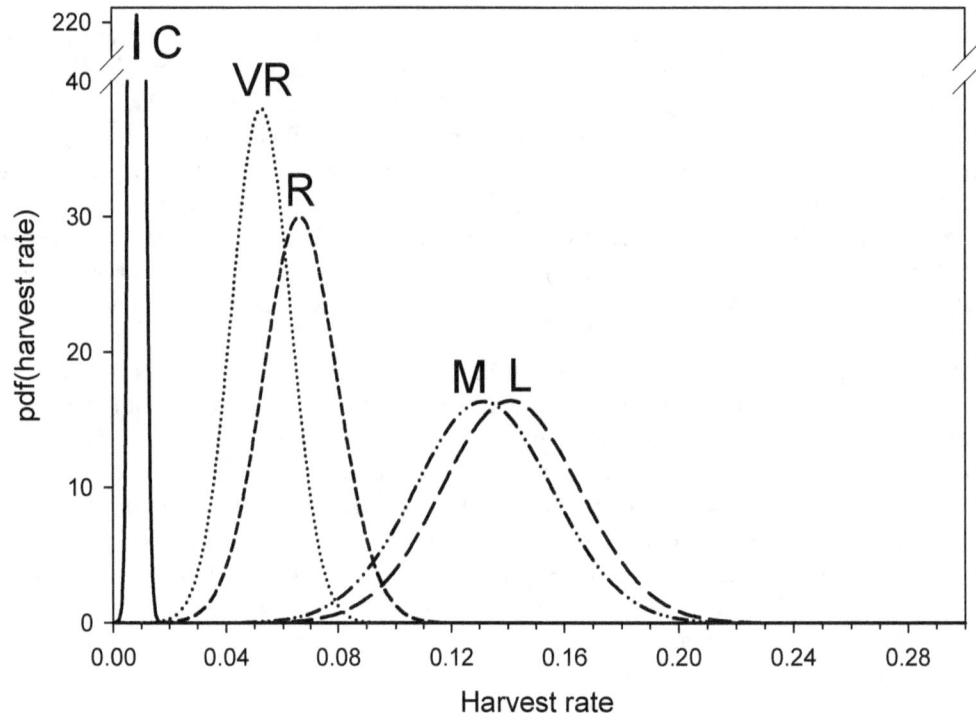

Fig. 5. Probability density functions (pdf) of harvest rates of adult male midcontinent mallards under current regulatory alternatives in the three western Flyways (C = closed season, VR = very restrictive, R = restrictive, M = moderate, L = liberal).

16

Table 9. Predicted harvest rates of adult male eastern mallards based on regulations in the Atlantic Flyway. The parameter μ is the mean harvest rate expected in the absence of framework-date extensions and Δ is the marginal change in mean harvest rate expected with extended framework dates. Standard errors are in parentheses.

Regulatory alternative	μ	Δ	$\mu + \Delta$
Closed (U.S.)	0.0800 (0.0240)	N/A	
Very restrictive	0.1212 (0.0364)	N/A	
Restrictive	0.1352 (0.0406)	N/A	
Moderate	0.1625 (0.0488)	0.01 (0.01)	0.1725 (0.0498)
Liberal	0.1771 (0.0531)	0.01 (0.01)	0.1871 (0.0540)

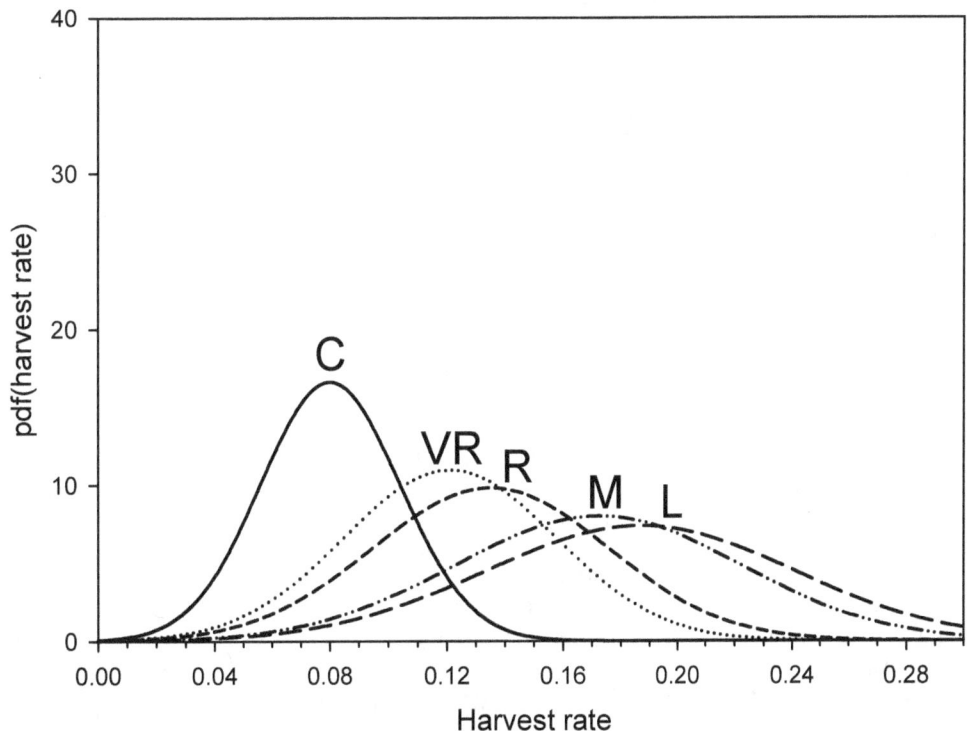

Fig. 6. Probability density functions (pdf) of harvest rates of adult male eastern mallards under current regulatory alternatives in the Atlantic Flyway (C = closed, VR = very restrictive, R = restrictive, M = moderate, L = liberal).

OPTIMAL REGULATORY STRATEGIES

The optimal regulatory strategy for the three western Flyways was derived using: (1) the 2002 regulatory alternatives; (2) the revised population models and associated weights for midcontinent mallards; and (3) the dual objectives to maximize long-term cumulative harvest and achieve a population goal of 8.799 million midcontinent mallards. The resulting regulatory strategy (Fig. 7 and Table 10) is somewhat more conservative and knife-edged than that used last year (USFWS 2001). Assuming that regulatory choices adhered to this strategy, the harvest value and breeding-population size would be expected to average 1.02 (SD = 0.85) million and 7.10 (SD = 1.56) million, respectively. Note that prescriptions for closed seasons in this strategy and others in this report represent resource conditions that are insufficient to support one of the current regulatory alternatives, given current harvest-management objectives. However, closed seasons under all of these conditions are not necessarily required for long-term resource protection, and simply reflect the constraints of the NAWMP population goal and the current regulatory alternatives.

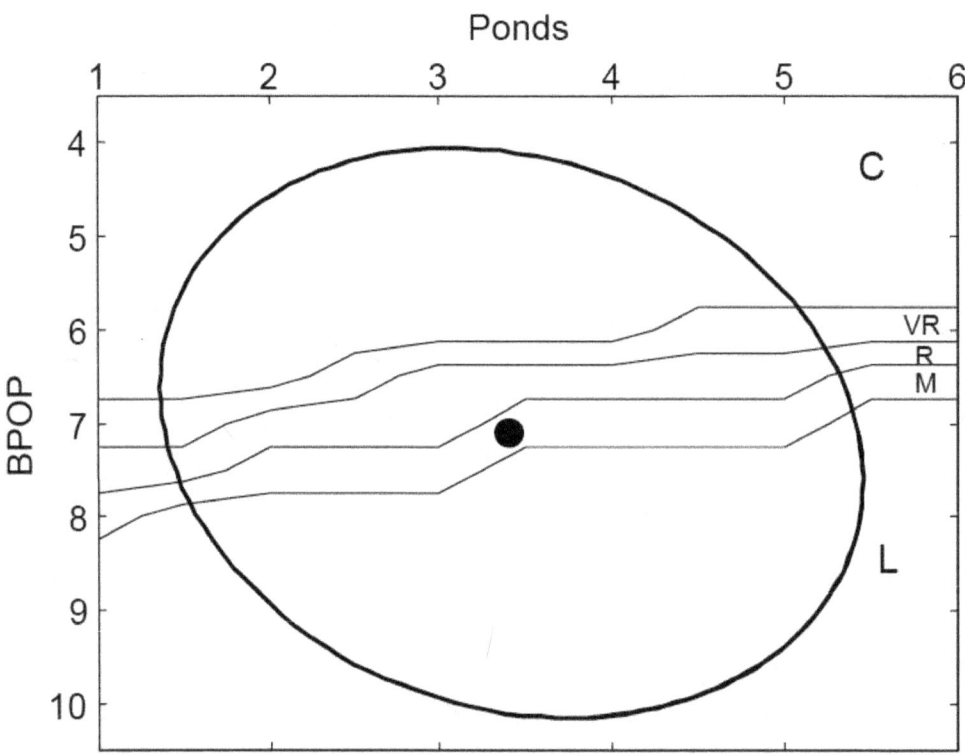

Fig. 7. Optimal regulatory choices in the three western Flyways for the 2002 hunting season conditioned on population size (BPOP) and pond numbers in Prairie Canada. This strategy is based on current regulatory alternatives (with framework-date extensions), on the revised midcontinent-mallard models and weights, and on the dual objectives of maximizing long-term cumulative harvest and achieving a population goal of 8.799 million mallards. The dot in the center of the figure represents predicted mean population size and pond numbers under this strategy and combination of model weights, and the ellipse represents conditions expected in 95% of all years. (C = closed season, VR = very restrictive, R = restrictive, M = moderate, L = liberal)

Based on a midcontinent population size of 8.5 million mallards (traditional surveys plus MN, MI, and WI) and 1.44 million ponds in Prairie Canada, the optimal regulatory choice for the Pacific, Central, and Mississippi Flyways in 2002 is the liberal alternative.

Table 10. Optimal regulatory choices[a] in the three western Flyways for the 2002 hunting season. This strategy is based on current regulatory alternatives (with framework-date extensions), on the revised midcontinent-mallard models and weights, and on the dual objectives of maximizing long-term cumulative harvest and achieving a population goal of 8.799 million mallards. The shaded cell represents the prescribed regulatory choice for 2002.

Mallards[c]	Ponds[b]										
	1.0	1.5	2.0	2.5	3.0	3.5	4.0	4.5	5.0	5.5	6.0
≤5.5	C	C	C	C	C	C	C	C	C	C	C
6.0	C	C	C	C	C	C	C	VR	VR	VR	VR
6.5	C	C	C	VR	R	R	R	R	R	M	M
7.0	R	R	R	R	R	M	M	M	M	L	L
7.5	R	R	M	M	M	L	L	L	L	L	L
8.0	M	L	L	L	L	L	L	L	L	L	L
≥8.5	L	L	L	L	L	L	L	L	L	L	L

[a] C = closed season, VR = very restrictive, R = restrictive, M = moderate, and L = liberal.
[b] Estimated number of ponds in Prairie Canada in May, in millions.
[c] Estimated number of midcontinent mallards during May, in millions.

We optimized the regulatory choice for the Atlantic Flyway based on: (1) current regulatory alternatives; (2) the revised population models and associated weights for eastern mallards; and (3) an objective to maximize long-term cumulative harvest. The resulting strategy suggests liberal regulations for all population sizes of record, and is characterized by a lack of intermediate regulations (Table 11). The strategy exhibits this behavior largely because of the small differences in harvest rate among regulatory alternatives (Fig. 6).

Table 11. Optimal regulatory choices[a] in the Atlantic Flyway for the 2002 hunting season. This strategy is based on current regulatory alternatives (with framework-date extensions), on the revised eastern-mallard models and weights, and on an objective to maximize long-term cumulative harvest. The shaded cell represents the prescribed regulatory choice for 2002.

Mallards[b]	Regulation
≤200	C
225	VR
250	R
275	M
≥300	L

[a] C = closed season, VR = very restrictive, R = restrictive, M = moderate, and L = liberal.
[b] Estimated number of eastern mallards in the combined federal and state surveys, in thousands.

We simulated the use of the regulatory strategy in Table 11 to determine expected performance characteristics. Assuming that harvest management adhered to this strategy, the annual harvest and breeding population size would be expected to average 478 (SD = 128) thousand and 880 (SD = 175) thousand, respectively.

Based on a breeding population size of 1.0 million mallards, the optimal regulatory choice for the Atlantic Flyway in 2002 is the liberal alternative.

Strategic Issues in AHM

Policy Questions

The AHM Working Group has begun a strategic discussion about future development and application of AHM. This discussion was motivated in part by the special session on AHM that was held at the 2000 North American Wildlife and Natural Resources Conference (Humburg et al. 2000, Johnson and Case 2000, Nichols 2000). That session offered a retrospective on the development of AHM, and described a number of policy issues affecting future progress. Relevant questions that need to be addressed include:

(a) Should AHM account explicitly for hunter "satisfaction" and, if so, how would it be measured and monitored? What constitutes a "fair" distribution of harvest or hunting opportunity, and should regulations be used to achieve this fairness?

(b) To what extent should the population goals of the North American Waterfowl Management Plan influence hunting opportunity?

(c) To date, AHM has been based on mallards. To what extent should the USFWS try to account for differences in the harvest potential of various duck stocks in setting hunting regulations? How does the USFWS distinguish what is desirable from what is practical?

(d) How many regulatory alternatives should there be? Among the alternatives, what are desirable or acceptable ranges of season lengths, bag limits, and framework dates? How often should the set of regulatory alternatives be reviewed?

The USFWS has decided to convene a task force, comprised of recognized state and federal leaders in waterfowl management, to help address these and other questions related to future application of AHM. This task force will need to work closely with the USFWS, the AHM Working Group, and the Wildlife Management Institute (WMI). The WMI has received federal aid to help explore the relationship between waterfowl hunting regulations and hunter satisfaction and participation, and to recommend how such information might be used in the AHM process.

Multi-Species Harvest Management

Variation is a defining feature of ecological systems. Virtually all ecological systems exhibit a broad range of variation on temporal, spatial, and organizational (e.g., taxonomic) scales, ultimately as a function of how individual organisms respond to their environment (Levin 1992). The scales at which individuals are aggregated for management purposes is an arbitrary decision, but one that can strongly influence both the benefits and costs of management (Johnson and Williams 1999). Management systems that account for important sources of ecological variation are expected to yield the highest benefits, but also are likely to be characterized by relatively high monitoring and assessment costs (Babcock and Sparrowe 1989, Sparrowe 1990).

One of the most difficult scale issues confronting AHM concerns that of multiple duck species. The problem is characterized by the following features:

(1) duck species vary in their potential to support sport harvest;

(2) multiple species generally are exposed to a common hunting season (although species-specific harvests can be regulated within limits by stratifying hunting regulations on spatial, temporal, and organizational scales);

(3) species-specific harvest returns and population trajectories are subject to considerable uncertainty, whose sources include uncontrolled environmental variation, random effects of regulations (i.e., partial controllability), uncertainties in population dynamics, and errors and biases in data-collection programs (i.e., partial observability); and

(4) management objectives are complex, in that they must account for species-specific values (i.e., not all species will be equally valued by hunters) and for the legal mandate to prevent over-exploitation of any particular species.

It is increasingly apparent that the future development and success of AHM will depend heavily on how we address the multi-species problem. There are several challenges, however, that won't be overcome easily. First, although AHM provides a coherent framework for exploring the effects of various approaches to multi-species harvesting, those explorations can be

20

conducted only to the extent that information on the dynamics of potential stocks is available. And while AHM provides an effective means for coping with uncertainty, high levels of uncertainty in management outcomes will severely reduce the benefits expected from an explicit recognition of variation in harvest potential. Second, more objective decisions about the appropriate multi-species approach will require a full accounting of monitoring and assessment costs. There also may be social costs to consider as regulations become increasingly complex to account for variation in harvest potential. Third, there will be difficult decisions about harvest-management objectives, including the importance of population goals, the relative value of species among hunters, and what constitutes fair allocations of hunting opportunity.

LITERATURE CITED

Babcock, K. M., and R. D. Sparrowe. 1989. Balancing expectations with reality in duck harvest management. Transactions of the North American Wildlife and Natural Resources Conference 54:594-599.

Blohm, R. J. 1989. Introduction to harvest - understanding surveys and season setting. Proceedings of the International Waterfowl Symposium 6:118-133.

Burnham, K. P., G. C. White, and D. R. Anderson. 1984. Estimating the effect of hunting on annual survival rates of adult mallards. Journal of Wildlife Management 48:350-361.

Heusman, H W, and J. R. Sauer. 2000. The northeastern states' waterfowl breeding population survey. Wildlife Society Bulletin 28:355-364.

Humburg, D. D., T. W. Aldrich, S. Baker, G. Costanzo, J. H. Gammonley, M. A. Johnson, B. Swift, and D. Yparraguirre. 2000. Adaptive harvest management: has anything really changed? Transactions of the North American Wildlife and Natural Resources Conference 65:78-93.

Johnson, F. A., and D. J. Case. 2000. Adaptive regulation of waterfowl harvests: lessons learned and prospects for the future. Transactions of the North American Wildlife and Natural Resources Conference. 65:94-108.

Johnson, F. A., J. A. Dubovsky, M. C. Runge, and D. R. Eggeman. 2002a. A revised protocol for the adaptive harvest management of eastern mallards. Fish and Wildlife Service, U.S. Dept. Interior, Washington, D.C. 13pp.

Johnson, F. A., W. L. Kendall, and J. A. Dubovsky. 2002b. Conditions and limitations on learning in the adaptive management of mallard harvests. Wildlife Society Bulletin 30:176-185.

Johnson, F. A., C. T. Moore, W. L. Kendall, J. A. Dubovsky, D. F. Caithamer, J. R. Kelley, Jr., and B. K. Williams. 1997. Uncertainty and the management of mallard harvests. Journal of Wildlife Management 61:202-216.

Johnson, F. A., J. A. Royle, and M. C. Runge. 2002c. Framework-date extensions and the adaptive management of mallard harvests. Fish and Wildlife Service, U.S. Dept. Interior, Washington, D.C. 10pp.

Johnson, F. A., and B. K. Williams. 1999. Protocol and practice in the adaptive management of waterfowl harvests. Conservation Ecology 3(1): 8. [online] URL: http://www.consecol.org/vol3/iss1/art8.

Johnson, F. A., B. K. Williams, J. D. Nichols, J. E. Hines, W. L. Kendall, G. W. Smith, and D. F. Caithamer. 1993. Developing an adaptive management strategy for harvesting waterfowl in North America. Transactions of the North American Wildlife and Natural Resources Conference 58:565-583.

Johnson, F. A., B. K. Williams, and P. R. Schmidt. 1996. Adaptive decision-making in waterfowl harvest and habitat management. Proceedings of the International Waterfowl Symposium 7:26-33.

Levin, S. 1992. The problem of pattern and scale in ecology. Ecology 73:1943-1967.

Lubow, B. C. 1995. SDP: Generalized software for solving stochastic dynamic optimization problems. Wildlife Society Bulletin 23:738-742.

Miller, M. W. 2000. Modeling annual mallard production in the prairie-parkland region. Journal of Wildlife Management 64:561-575.

Munro, R. E., and C. F. Kimball. 1982. Population ecology of the mallard. VII. Distribution and derivation of the harvest. U.S. Fish and Wildlife Service Resource Publication 147. 127pp.

Nichols, J. D. 2000. Evolution of harvest management for North American waterfowl: selective pressures and preadaptations for adaptive harvest management. Transactions of the North American Wildlife and Natural Resources Conference 65:65-77.

Nichols, J. D., F. A. Johnson, and B. K. Williams. 1995. Managing North American waterfowl in the face of uncertainty. Annual Review of Ecology and Systematics 26:177-199.

Runge, M. C., F. A. Johnson, J. A. Dubovsky, W. L. Kendall, J. Lawrence, and J. Gammonley. 2002. A revised protocol for the adaptive harvest management of midcontinent mallards. Fish and Wildlife Service, U.S. Dept. Interior, Washington, D.C. 28pp.

Schafer, J. L. 1997. Analysis of incomplete multivariate data. Chapman and Hall, London. 430pp.

Sparrowe, R. D. 1990. Developing harvest regulations strategies for wood ducks. Pages 373-375 in Fredrickson, L. H., G. V. Burger, S. P. Havera, D. A. Graber, R. E. Kirby, and T. S. Taylor, eds., Proceedings of the 1988 North American Wood Duck Symposium, St. Louis, Missouri.

U.S. Fish and Wildlife Service. 2000a. Adaptive harvest management: 2000 duck hunting season. U.S. Dept. Interior, Washington. D.C. 43pp.

U.S. Fish and Wildlife Service. 2000b. Framework-date extensions for duck hunting in the United States: projected impacts & coping with uncertainty, U.S. Dept. Interior, Washington, D.C. 8pp

U.S. Fish and Wildlife Service. 2001. Adaptive harvest management: 2001 duck hunting season. U.S. Dept. Interior, Washington. D.C. 47pp.

Walters, C. J. 1986. Adaptive management of renewable resources. MacMillan Publ. Co., New York, N.Y. 374pp.

Williams, B. K., and F. A. Johnson. 1995. Adaptive management and the regulation of waterfowl harvests. Wildlife Society Bulletin 23:430-436.

Williams, B. K., F. A. Johnson, and K. Wilkins. 1996. Uncertainty and the adaptive management of waterfowl harvests. Journal of Wildlife Management 60:223-232.

APPENDIX A: AHM Working Group

Scott Baker
Dept. of Wildlife, Fisheries, & Parks
P.O. Box 378
Redwood, MS 39156
 phone: 601-661-0294
fax: 601-364-2209
e-mail: mahannah1@aol.com

Bob Blohm
U.S. Fish and Wildlife Service
Arlington Square, Room 634
4401 North Fairfax Drive,
Arlington, VA 22203
phone: 703-358-1966
fax: 703-358-2272
e-mail: robert_blohm@fws.gov

Brad Bortner
U.S. Fish and Wildlife Service
911 NE 11th Ave.
Portland, OR 97232-4181
phone: 503-231-6164
fax: 503-231-2364
e-mail: brad_bortner@fws.gov

Frank Bowers
U.S. Fish and Wildlife Service
1875 Century Blvd., Suite 345
Atlanta, GA 30345
phone: 404-679-7188
fax: 404-679-7285
e-mail: frank_bowers@fws.gov

Dave Case
D.J. Case & Associates
607 Lincolnway West
Mishawaka, IN 46544
phone: 574-258-0100
fax: 574-258-0189
e-mail: dave@djcase.com

Dale Caswell
Canadian Wildlife Service
123 Main St. Suite 150
Winnepeg, Manitoba, CANADA R3C 4W2
phone: 204-983-5260
fax: 204-983-5248
e-mail: dale.caswell@ec.gc.ca

John Cornely
U.S. Fish and Wildlife Service
P.O. Box 25486, DFC
Denver, CO 80225
phone: 303-236-8155 (ext 259)
fax: 303-236-8680
e-mail: john_cornely@fws.gov

Gary Costanzo
Dept. of Game and Inland Fisheries
5806 Mooretown Road
Williamsburg, VA 23188
phone: 757-253-4180
fax: 757-253-4182
e-mail: gcostanzo@dgif.state.va.us

Jim Dubovsky
U.S. Fish & Wildlife Service
P.O. Box 25486 DFC
Denver, CO 80225-0486
phone: 303-236-8155 (ext 238)
fax: 303-236-8680
e-mail: james_dubovsky@fws.gov

Diane Eggeman
Fish & Wildlife Conservation Commission
8932 Apalachee Pkwy.
Tallahassee, FL 32311
phone: 850-488-5878
fax: 850-488-5884
e-mail: eggemadr@fwc.state.fl.us

Ken Gamble
U.S. Fish and Wildlife Service
608 Cherry Street, Room 119
Columbia, MO 65201
phone: 573-876-1915
fax: 573-876-1917
e-mail: ken_gamble@fws.gov

Jim Gammonley
Division of Wildlife
317 West Prospect
Fort Collins, CO 80526
phone: 970-472-4379
fax: 970-472-4457
e-mail: jim.gammonley@state.co.us

Pam Garrettson
U.S. Fish & Wildlife service
11500 American Holly Drive
Laurel, MD 20708-4016
phone: 301-497-5865
fax: 301-497-5871
e-mail: pam_garrettson@fws.gov

George Haas
U.S. Fish and Wildlife Service
300 Westgate Center Drive
Hadley, MA 01035-9589
phone: 413-253-8576
fax: 413-253-8480
e-mail: george_haas@fws.gov

Jeff Haskins
U.S. Fish and Wildlife Service
P.O. Box 1306
Albuquerque, NM 87103
phone: 505-248-6827 (ext 30)
fax: 505-248-7885
e-mail: jeff_haskins@fws.gov

Mark Herzog
Dept. Environmental & Resource Sciences
University of Nevada
Reno, NV 89512
phone: 775-784-6558
e-mail: mherzog@unr.edu

Dale Humburg
Dept. of Conservation
Fish & Wildlife Research Center
1110 South College Ave.
Columbia, MO 65201
phone: 573-882-9880 (ext 3246)
fax: 573-882-4517
e-mail: humbud@mail.conservation.state.mo.us

Fred Johnson
U.S. Fish & Wildlife Service
7920 NW 71st Street
Gainesville, FL 32653
phone: 352-378-8181 (ext 372)
fax: 352-378-4956
e-mail: fred_a_johnson@fws.gov

Mike Johnson
Game and Fish Department
100 North Bismarck Expressway
Bismarck, ND 58501-5095
phone: 701-328-6319
fax: 701-328-6352
e-mail: mjohnson@state.nd.us

Jim Kelley
U.S. Fish and Wildlife Service
BH Whipple Federal Building, 1 Federal Drive
Fort Snelling, MN 55111-4056
phone: 612-713-5409
fax: 612-713-5286
e-mail: james_r_kelley@fws.gov

Bill Kendall
U.S.G.S. Patuxent Wildlife Research Center
11510 American Holly Drive
Laurel, MD 20708-4017
phone: 301-497-5868
fax: 301-497-5666
e-mail: william_kendall@usgs.gov

Don Kraege
Dept. of Fish & Wildlife
600 Capital Way North
Olympia. WA 98501-1091
phone: 360-902-2509
fax: 360-902-2162
e-mail: kraegdkk@dfw.wa.gov

Jeff Lawrence
Dept. of Natural Resources
102 23rd St. NE
Bemidji, MN 56601
phone: 218-755-3910
fax: 218-755-2604
e-mail: jeff.lawrence@dnr.state.mn.us

Bob Leedy
U.S. Fish and Wildlife Service
1011 East Tudor Road
Anchorage, AK 99503-6119
phone: 907-786-3446
fax: 907-786-3641
e-mail: robert_leedy@fws.gov

Mary Moore
U.S. Fish & Wildlife Service
206 Concord Drive
Watkinsville, GA 30677
phone: 706-769-2359
fax: 706-769-2359
e-mail: mary_moore@fws.gov

Jim Nichols
U.S.G.S. Patuxent Wildlife Research Center
11510 American Holly Drive
Laurel, MD 20708-4017
phone: 301-497-5660
fax: 301-497-5666
e-mail: jim_nichols@usgs.gov

Mark Otto
U.S. Fish & Wildlife Service
11500 American Holly Drive
Laurel, MD 20708-4016
phone: 301-497-5872
fax: 301-497-5871
e-mail: mark_otto@fws.gov

Paul Padding
U.S. Fish & Wildlife Service
10815 Loblolly Pine Drive
Laurel, MD 20708-4028
phone: 301-497-5980
fax: 301-497-5981
e-mail: paul_padding@fws.gov

Michael C. Runge
U.S.G.S. Patuxent Wildlife Research Center
11510 American Holly Drive
Laurel, MD 20708-4017
phone: 301-497-5748
fax: 301-497-5666
e-mail: michael_runge@usgs.gov

Jerry Serie
U.S. Fish & Wildlife Service
12100 Beech Forest Road
Laurel, MD 20708-4038
phone: 301-497-5851
fax: 301-497-5885
e-mail: jerry_serie@fws.gov

Dave Sharp
U.S. Fish and Wildlife Service
P.O. Box 25486, DFC
Denver, CO 80225-0486
phone: 303-275-2386
fax: 303-275-2384
e-mail: dave_sharp@fws.gov

Sue Sheaffer
Coop. Fish & Wildl. Research Unit
Fernow Hall, Cornell University
Ithaca, NY 14853
phone: 607-255-2837
fax: 607-255-1895
e-mail: ses11@cornell.edu

Graham Smith
U.S. Fish & Wildlife Service
11500 American Holly Drive
Laurel, MD 20708-4016
phone: 301-497-5860
fax: 301-497-5871
e-mail: graham_smith@fws.gov

Bob Trost
U.S. Fish and Wildlife Service
911 NE 11th Ave.
Portland, OR 97232-4181
phone: 503-231-6162
fax: 503-231-6228
e-mail: robert_trost@fws.gov

Khristi Wilkins
U.S. Fish & Wildlife Service
11500 American Holly Drive
Laurel, MD 20708-4016
phone: 301-497-5557
fax: 301-497-5971
e-mail: khristi_a_wilkins@fws.gov

Ken Williams
U.S.G.S. Cooperative Research Units
12201 Sunrise Valley Drive
Mail Stop 303
Reston, VA 20192
phone: 703-648-4260
fax: 703-648-4269
e-mail: byron_ken_williams@usgs.gov

Dan Yparraguirre
Dept. of Fish & Game
1812 Ninth Street
Sacramento, CA 95814
phone: 916-445-3685
e-mail: dyparraguirre@dfg.ca.gov

Appendix B: Regulatory Alternatives for the 1995 and 1996 Hunting Seasons

Regulation	Flyway			
	Atlantic	Mississippi	Central[a]	Pacific[b]
Shooting hours	one-half hour before sunrise to sunset			
Framework dates	Oct 1 - Jan 20	Saturday closest to October 1 and Sunday closest to January 20		
Season length (days)				
Restrictive	30	30	39	59
Moderate	40	40	51	79
Liberal	50	50	60	93
Bag limit (total / mallard / female mallard)				
Restrictive	3 / 3 / 1	3 / 2 / 1	3 / 3 / 1	4 / 3 / 1
Moderate	4 / 4 / 1	4 / 3 / 1	4 / 4 / 1	5 / 4 / 1
Liberal	5 / 5 / 1	5 / 4 / 1	5 / 5 / 1	6-7[c] / 6-7[c] / 1

[a] The High Plains Mallard Management Unit was allowed 12, 16, and 23 extra days under the restrictive, moderate, and liberal alternatives, respectively.
[b] The Columbia Basin Mallard Management Unit was allowed seven extra days under all three alternatives.
[c] The limits were 6 in 1995 and 7 in 1996.

APPENDIX C: Predicting Harvest Rates

This procedure involves: (1) linear models that predict total seasonal mallard harvest for varying regulations (daily bag limit and season length), while accounting for trends in numbers of successful duck hunters; and (2) use of these models to adjust historical estimates of mallard harvest rates to reflect differences in bag limit, season length and trends in hunter numbers. Using historical data from both the U.S. Waterfowl Mail Questionnaire and Parts Collection Surveys, and with the use of several key assumptions, the resulting models allowed us to predict total seasonal mallard harvest and associated predicted harvest rates for varying combinations of season length and daily bag limits.

Total seasonal mallard harvest is predicted using two separate models: the "harvest" model which predicts average daily mallard harvest per successful duck hunter for each day of the hunting season (Table C-1), and the "hunter" model which predicts the number of successful duck hunters (Table C-2). The "harvest" model uses as the dependent variable the square root of the average daily mallard harvest (per successful duck hunter). The independent variables include the consecutive day of the hunting season (splits were ignored), daily mallard bag limit, season length, and the interaction of bag limit and season length. Also included is an effect representing the opening day (of the first split), an effect representing a week (7 day) effect, and several other interaction terms. Seasonal mallard harvest per successful duck hunter is obtained by back-transforming the predicted values that resulted from the model, and summing the average daily harvest over the season length. The "hunter" model uses information on the numbers of successful duck hunters (based on duck stamp sales information) from 1981-95. Using daily bag limit and season length as independent variables, the number of successful duck hunters is predicted for each state.

Both the "harvest" and "hunter" models were developed for each of seven management areas: the Atlantic Flyway portion with compensatory days (AF-COMP); the Atlantic Flyway portion without compensatory days (AF-NOCOMP); the Mississippi Flyway (MF); the low plains portion of Central Flyway (CF-lp); the High Plains Mallard Management Unit in the Central Flyway (CF-HP); the Columbia Basin Mallard Management Unit in the Pacific Flyway (PF-CB); and the remainder of the Pacific Flyway excluding Alaska (PF). The numbers of successful hunters predicted at the state level are summed to obtain a total number (H) for each management area. Likewise, the "harvest" model results in a seasonal mallard harvest per successful duck hunter (A) for each management area. Total seasonal mallard harvest (T) is formed by the product of H and A.

To compare total seasonal mallard harvest under different regulatory alternatives, ratios of T are formed for each management area and then combined into a weighted mean. *Under the key assumption that the ratio of harvest rates realized under two different regulatory alternatives is equal to the expected ratio of total harvest obtained under the same two alternatives*, the harvest rate experienced under the historic "liberal" package (1979-84) was adjusted by T to produce predicted harvest rates for the current regulatory alternatives.

The models developed here were not designed, nor are able, to predict mallard harvest rates directly. The procedure relies heavily on statistical and conceptual models that must meet certain assumptions. We have no way to verify these assumptions, nor can we gauge their effects should they not be met. The use of this procedure for predicting mallard harvest rates for regulations alternatives for which we have little or no experience warrants considerable caution.

Table C-1. Parameter estimates by management area for models of seasonal harvest per successful hunter.[a]

Model effect[a]	AF- COMP.	AF-NOCOMP	MF	CF-lp	CF-HP	PF-CB	PF
INTERCEPT	0.378359	0.555790	0.485971	0.554667	0.593799	0.736258	0.543791
(SE)	(0.061477)	(0.134516)	(0.037175)	(0.041430)	(0.059649)	(0.154315)	(0.054712)
OPEN	0.194945	0.263793	0.175012	0.092507	0.113074	0.361696	0.322255
(SE)	(0.010586)	(0.018365)	(0.011258)	(0.015623)	(0.018530)	(0.040605)	(0.012730)
WEEK	0.024232	0.040392	-0.016479	-0.108472	-0.074895	-0.063422	-0.060477
(SE)	(0.006561)	(0.011436)	(0.006965)	(0.008860)	(0.009437)	(0.018220)	(0.006118)
WEEK2	-0.003586	-0.006823	0.000422	0.010472	0.006782	0.003573	0.004893
(SE)	(0.000796)	(0.001392)	(0.000847)	(0.001075)	(0.001150)	(0.002266)	(0.000746)
WK*SDAY	-0.001245	-0.001395	-0.000073	0.002578	0.001222	-0.000102	0.000116
(SE)	(0.000231)	(0.000407)	(0.000248)	(0.000260)	(0.000215)	(0.000289)	(0.000120)
WK2*SDAY	0.000163	0.000219	0.000052	-0.000271	-0.000109	0.000045	0.000007
(SE)	(0.000028)	(0.000050)	(0.000030)	(0.000032)	(0.000026)	(0.000037)	(0.000015)
SEASDAY	0.000419	-0.001034	-0.002559	-0.006322	-0.003174	-0.000615	-0.000909
(SE)	(0.000407)	(0.000712)	(0.000434)	(0.000464)	(0.000382)	(0.000476)	(0.000209)
MALBAG	-0.025557	-0.062755	0.026729	0.016049	-0.029753	-0.049532	-0.021774
(SE)	(0.019282)	(0.043020)	(0.015007)	(0.010766)	(0.013918)	(0.047903)	(0.017457)
SEASLEN	-0.004852	-0.008836	-0.004869	-0.001250	-0.003089	0.001562	-0.001931
(SE)	(0.001260)	(0.002750)	(0.000768)	(0.000833)	(0.000995)	(0.001682)	(0.000591)
BAG*SEAS	0.000926	0.002018	0.000332	-0.000033	0.000732	0.000024	0.000328
(SE)	(0.000393)	(0.000877)	(0.000310)	(0.000202)	(0.000216)	(0.000464)	(0.000184)

[a]Model effect	Description
INTERCEPT	Intercept
OPEN	Opening Day of First Split (Y,N)
WEEK	Day of Week (1,2,3,4,5,6,7)
WEEK2	Week * Week (Quadratic Effect)
WK*SDAY	Week * Day of Season Interaction
WK2*SDAY	Week * Week * Day of Season Interaction
SEASDAY	Day of Season (Consecutive)
MALBAG	Daily Mallard Bag Limit
SEASLEN	Season Length
BAG*SEAS	Daily Mallard Bag Limit * Season Length Interaction

Table C-2. Parameter estimates by management area for models to predict hunter numbers.

Mgmt Area	Effect	State/Zone	Estimate	SE	Mgmt Area	Effect	State/Zone	Estimate	SE
AF-Comp.	MALBAG		-229.854	320.613	CF - lp	MALBAG		577.848	715.617
	SEASLEN		119.595	28.473		SEASLEN		317.973	100.931
	Intercepts:	CT	925.275	823.888		Intercepts:	KS	-6,006.131	3,108.375
		DE	376.732	829.784			NE	-4,997.796	3,114.451
		ME	3,581.062	825.956			ND	-3,930.604	3,021.002
		MD	10,712.000	809.333			OK	-8,010.002	3,208.936
		NJ	5,940.028	813.652			SD	-4,053.537	3,021.002
		NC	12,798.000	836.186			TX	33,480.000	3,021.002
		PA	17,683.000	822.566	CF - HP	MALBAG		734.041	181.624
		VA	7,276.371	809.333		SEASLEN		-1.332	16.318
		WV	-2,884.782	818.825		Intercepts:	CO	12,354.000	687.696
		MA_3	1,679.885	818.507			KS	-973.654	688.526
		MA_R	-336.288	843.081			MT	482.197	699.176
AF-No comp.	MALBAG		71.885	188.301			NE	3,222.880	688.526
	SEASLEN		62.574	18.776			NM	447.280	688.526
	Intercepts:	FL	9,709.872	530.458			ND	4,559.079	541.659
		GA	7,058.253	541.184			OK	-2,299.609	687.696
		RI	-1,515.873	543.352			SD	748.221	695.658
		SC	10,004.000	541.184			TX	2,817.864	695.658
		VT	679.453	541.184			WY	1,639.613	688.526
		NH_1	-1,536.280	541.184	PF - CB	MALBAG		505.129	411.451
		NH_2	201.430	536.395		SEASLEN		31.446	48.602
		NY_1	336.305	537.703		Intercepts:	OR	-3,910.659	2,311.323
		NY_2	-2,122.214	541.184			WA	5,433.261	2,334.479
		NY_5	7,070.786	541.184					
		NY_R	8,650.966	538.322					
		OH_1	-2,426.542	535.906					

Table C-2, continued.

Mgmt Area	Effect	State/Zone	Estimate	SE	Mgmt Area	Effect	State/Zone	Estimate	SE
MF	MALBAG		-4,523.798	1,231.622	PF	MALBAG		790.844	284.473
	SEASLEN		897.413	120.583		SEASLEN		59.303	31.696
	Intercepts:	AL	-15,044.000	2,361.763		Intercepts:	AZ	-3,958.814	1,402.487
		AR	5,599.384	2,361.763			CO	-4,832.461	1,400.722
		IL	7,438.650	2,361.763			ID	6,285.454	1,384.878
		IN	-13,932.000	2,361.763			MT	-887.114	1,458.939
		IA	-1,346.879	2,337.443			NV	-2,483.897	1,369.116
		KY	-15,477.000	2,394.393			NM	-7,588.133	1,395.432
		LA	41,690.000	2,543.303			OR	11,687.000	1,397.194
		MI	10,232.000	2,361.763			UT	6,803.640	1,415.495
		MN	61,174.000	2,635.798			WY	9,398.653	1,402.487
		MS	-9,207.288	2,285.436			CA_1	-3,696.948	1,385.102
		MO	-2,225.616	2,361.763			CA_2	-5,421.502	1,427.980
		TN	-6,958.016	2,361.763			CA_3	3,580.319	1,385.102
		WI	27,254.000	2,361.763			CA_4	-6,475.400	1,378.069
		OH_R	-9,163.989	2,635.798			CA_5	29,744.000	1,385.102

31

APPENDIX D: Updating Predictions of Harvest Rates

Statistical Procedures

We rely on standard Bayesian statistical techniques for updating predictions of regulation-specific harvest rates of mallards (Johnson et al. 2002c). We first specified the following model structure:

$$data: \quad y_t \sim Normal(h_t, \sigma_t^2)$$
$$truth: \quad h_t \sim Normal(\mu, v^2)$$

In this model, y_t represents an estimate (with sampling variance σ^2) of the annual harvest rate h_t under a given regulatory alternative. In turn, we assume that h_t is drawn from a normal distribution with mean μ and process error v^2. The process error represents the amount of variability in harvest rates under the same regulatory alternative due to annual variation in weather, habitat conditions, timing of migration, etc.

The problem is to estimate μ and v^2, given our prior beliefs about these parameters and any estimates of harvest rates y_t that become available from subsequent experience. To do this, we must specify prior distributions for the parameters μ and v^2. These distributions represent a quantitative statement of our prior beliefs about the mean and variance of the harvest rate expected under a given regulatory alternative. For the prior distribution of μ, we use:

$$\mu \sim Normal\left(\theta, \frac{v^2}{n}\right)$$

where

$$v^2 = (\theta \times 0.2)^2$$
$$n = 6$$

The parameter θ must be specified for each regulatory alternative. We use the predicted mean harvest rates derived from the procedures described in Appendix C and provided by USFWS (2000a:13-14). Those procedures, however, provide only a combined estimate of $v^2 + \sigma^2$, which is not useful for our purpose. Therefore, we relied on information provided by Johnson et al. (1997), who estimated that v is typically about 20% of the mean (i.e., CV = 0.2). We set $n = 6$ to reflect the empirical estimates of harvest rate during 1979-84 that were used to help derive initial predictions under the current regulatory alternatives.

Based on theoretical considerations, we suggest a scaled inverse gamma with n degrees of freedom and scale parameter v^2 for the prior distribution of v^2:

$$v^2 \sim Inverse\ Gamma\left(n, (\theta \times 0.2)^2\right)$$

Once prior distributions are fully specified for each regulatory alternative, they can be updated using estimates of harvest rates (based on band-recovery data) that become available after a particular regulatory alternative is implemented. Using standard Bayesian methodology, these prior distributions are converted to posterior distributions, from which sample posterior means and variances are derived. These posterior means and variances provide updated measures of μ and v^2, which are used for predictive purposes in the next cycle of regulation-setting.

Next, we modified the model structure to account for the marginal effect of framework-date extensions:

$$h_t' \sim Normal\left(\mu + \Delta, v^2\right)$$

where Δ is the absolute change in mean harvest rate. In this model we assume that the process error remains unaffected.

As before, a key question is what to use as a prior distribution for the parameter Δ. We use:

$$\Delta \sim Normal\left(\theta \times \rho,\ \phi^2\right)$$

where ρ is the expected proportional change in mean harvest rate, and the variance ϕ^2 is a measure of uncertainty about $(\theta \times \rho)$. A previous assessment suggests that $\rho = 0.15$ for midcontinent mallards and $\rho \leq 0.05$ for eastern mallards (USFWS 2000b). In the absence of other relevant assessments, we use these values for making initial predictions about the effects of framework-date extensions. Specifying ϕ^2 is more difficult because information provided by USFWS (2000b) is based on two critical assumptions: (1) that changes in harvest rate are proportional to changes in harvest; and (2) that past experience with an early opening date in Iowa and a late closing date in Mississippi accurately reflects the expected effect in other States where extensions have never been offered. Because of the tenuousness of these assumptions, we suggest that variance estimates presented by USFWS (2000b) do not adequately characterize the level of uncertainty about Δ. Therefore, we use values of ϕ^2 that bound a lower confidence limit for $(\theta \times \rho)$ by zero. This is an explicit recognition that our prior beliefs include the possibility that $\Delta = 0$.

When framework-date extensions are implemented, estimates of harvest rate derived from band-recovery data would be used to update the prior distribution for Δ. We note, however, that any inference about the causal relationship between Δ and framework extensions will be very weak because changes due to extensions will be confounded with any other uncontrolled changes in harvest rates (i.e., there will be no experimental controls).

Application to Midcontinent Mallards

We here demonstrate application of the Bayesian methods described above for updating predictions of harvest rates of midcontinent mallards under the liberal regulatory alternative without framework-date extensions. Based on analyses and assumptions described previously, we first specified prior distributions for μ and v^2:

$$\mu \sim Normal\left(0.1305, \frac{0.0261^2}{6}\right)$$

$$v^2 \sim Inverse\ Gamma\left(6, 0.0261^2\right)$$

We have estimates of harvest rate realized under the liberal alternative for the 1998 through 2001 hunting seasons. Reward banding in banding reference areas 2, 4, and 5 provided the basis for these estimates (USFWS 2001:40). Harvest rates in un-sampled reference areas were treated as missing, and conventional data augmentation techniques were used (Schafer 1997). Estimates of harvest rate were first computed for each reference area, and then these estimates were averaged using breeding-population estimates in each reference area as weights.

This procedure resulted in the following estimates:

$$y_{1998} = 0.108 \ (\sigma^2 = 0.013^2)$$
$$y_{1999} = 0.098 \ (\sigma^2 = 0.008^2)$$
$$y_{2000} = 0.129 \ (\sigma^2 = 0.011^2)$$
$$y_{2001} = 0.104 \ (\sigma^2 = 0.013^2)$$

Combining our prior distributions and these harvest-rate estimates, we calculated posterior (updated) means and standard deviations for the following parameters of interest:

$$h_{1998} = 0.112 \ (SD = 0.0111)$$
$$h_{1999} = 0.101 \ (SD = 0.0076)$$
$$h_{2000} = 0.127 \ (SD = 0.0100)$$
$$h_{2001} = 0.109 \ (SD = 0.0112)$$
$$\mu = 0.121 \quad (SD = 0.0082)$$
$$v^2 = 0.0222^2 \quad (SD = 0.00031)$$

Thus, our best estimate of the mean harvest rate (μ) under the liberal regulatory alternative (without framework-date extensions) decreased from 0.130 to 0.121 to become more consistent with the four years of observation. Also, the estimate of process error (v^2) decreased slightly to reflect the relatively low variability in harvest rates observed among the last four years.

NOTES